EDWARD HO

Pomegranate

SAN FRANCISCO

Pomegranate Communications, Inc.
Box 808022, Petaluma CA 94975
800 227 1428; www.pomegranate.com

Pomegranate Europe Ltd.
Unit 1, Heathcote Business Centre, Hurlbutt Road
Warwick, Warwickshire CV34 6TD, UK
[+44] 0 1926 430111; sales@pomeurope.co.uk

ISBN 978-0-7649-4110-8
Pomegranate Catalog No. AA399

Pomegranate publishes books of postcards on a wide range of subjects.
Please contact the publisher for more information.

Cover designed by Lora Santiago
Printed in Korea
16 15 14 13 12 11 10 09 08 07   10 9 8 7 6 5 4 3

To facilitate detachment of the postcards from this book, fold each card along its perforation line before tearing.

A stillness encloses the figures painted by Edward Hopper, and even the figures on his beloved sailboats stand motionless. Whether they sit in a late-night coffee shop, in a living room, on a train, the inhabitants of his pictures do not open to us: there is no question of psychology or insight: they could not be more alone. Hopper himself did not talk much. A friend of his reported, "Hopper had no small talk; he was famous for his monumental silences." Another writer described Hopper and his paintings as "uncouth, lonely and silent."

Smitten by American and European realism as a young man, Hopper (American, 1882–1967) did not find immediate success as a painter. Visits to Europe convinced him of his calling, but for many years he dwelt in obscurity, making his living by illustrating popular and trade magazines. Still, he belonged throughout this period to an artistic milieu, sharing a Greenwich Village apartment building with Edmund Wilson, John Dos Passos, and other writers and artists; one of his great heroes, Thomas Eakins, had lived at the same address. And throughout this early period he painted, drew, and etched.

No sooner had Hopper been recognized as one of twentieth-century America's great artists than the Abstract Expressionists seized the attention of critics and the public. This is just as well, since his strongly delineated late afternoon scenes seem inimical to a life lived in the public eye.

EDWARD HOPPER (AMERICAN, 1882–1967)

Room in Brooklyn, 1932
Oil on canvas, 74 x 86.4 cm (29⅛ x 34 in.)
Museum of Fine Arts, Boston
The Hayden Collection–Charles Henry Hayden Fund 35.66

BOX 808022   PETALUMA   CA 94975

Pomegranate

EDWARD HOPPER (AMERICAN, 1882–1967)

Nighthawks, 1942
Oil on canvas, 84.1 x 152.4 cm (33⅛ x 60 in.)
Friends of American Art Collection, 1942.51

BOX 808022   PETALUMA   CA 94975

Pomegranate

EDWARD HOPPER (AMERICAN, 1882–1967)

New York Movie, 1939
Oil on canvas, 81.9 x 101.9 cm (32¼ x 40⅛ in.)
Given anonymously (396.1941)
The Museum of Modern Art, New York

CA 94975 PETALUMA BOX 808022

Pomegranate

EDWARD HOPPER (AMERICAN, 1882–1967)

First Branch of the White River, Vermont, 1938
Watercolor over graphite pencil on paper,
55.2 x 68.3 cm (21¾ x 26⅞ in.)
Museum of Fine Arts, Boston
William Emerson Fund 39.43

BOX 808022   PETALUMA   CA 94975

Pomegranate

EDWARD HOPPER (AMERICAN, 1882–1967)

The Mansard Roof, 1923
Watercolor over graphite on paper,
35.2 x 50.8 cm (13⅞ x 20 in.)
Brooklyn Museum
Museum Collection Fund 23.100

BOX 808022   PETALUMA   CA 94975

Pomegranate

EDWARD HOPPER (AMERICAN, 1882–1967)

Gloucester Mansion, 1924
Watercolor on paper, 34 x 49.6 cm (13⅜ x 19½ in.)
Museum of Fine Arts, Boston
Bequest of John T. Spaulding 48.717

CA 94975 PETALUMA BOX 808022

Pomegranate

EDWARD HOPPER (AMERICAN, 1882–1967)

Tables for Ladies, 1930
Oil on canvas, 122.6 x 153 cm (48¼ x 60¼ in.)
The Metropolitan Museum of Art, New York City
George A. Hearn Fund, 1931 (31.62)

BOX 808022 PETALUMA CA 94975

Pomegranate

EDWARD HOPPER (AMERICAN, 1882–1967)

Lighthouse and Buildings, Portland Head,
Cape Elizabeth, Maine, 1927
Watercolor over graphite pencil on paper,
34.3 x 49.5 cm (13½ x 19½ in.)
Museum of Fine Arts, Boston
Bequest of John T. Spaulding 48.723

CA 94975

PETALUMA

BOX 808022

Pomegranate

EDWARD HOPPER (AMERICAN, 1882–1967)

New York Restaurant, c. 1922
Oil on canvas, 61 x 76.2 cm (24 x 30 in.)
Collection of the Muskegon Museum of Art, Michigan
Hackley Picture Fund Purchase 1936.12

BOX 808022   PETALUMA   CA 94975

Pomegranate

EDWARD HOPPER (AMERICAN, 1882–1967)

Ground Swell, 1939
Oil on canvas, 91.9 x 127.2 cm (36³⁄₁₆ x 50¹⁄₁₆ in.)
Corcoran Gallery of Art, Washington, DC
Museum Purchase, William A. Clark Fund 43.6

BOX 808022 PETALUMA CA 94975

Pomegranate

EDWARD HOPPER (AMERICAN, 1882–1967)

Night Windows, 1928
Oil on canvas, 73.7 x 86.4 cm (29 x 34 in.)
Gift of John Hay Whitney (248.1940)
The Museum of Modern Art, New York

BOX 808022   PETALUMA   CA 94975

Pomegranate

EDWARD HOPPER (AMERICAN, 1882–1967)

Houses of Squam Light, Gloucester, 1923
Watercolor on paper, 28.6 x 44.3 cm (11¼ x 17⁷⁄₁₆ in.)
Museum of Fine Arts, Boston
Bequest of John T. Spaulding 48.716

CA 94975

PETALUMA

BOX 808022

Pomegranate

EDWARD HOPPER (AMERICAN, 1882–1967)

Cottages at North Truro, 1938
Watercolor on paper, 52.9 x 71.4 cm (20³⁄₁₆ x 28⅛ in.)
Collection of Barney A. Ebsworth

BOX 808022   PETALUMA   CA 94975

Pomegranate

EDWARD HOPPER (AMERICAN, 1882–1967)

Summertime, 1943
Oil on canvas, 74 x 111.8 cm (29⅛ x 44 in.)
Delaware Art Museum, Wilmington, Delaware
Gift of Dora Sexton Brown, 1962 (1962-28)

BOX 808022   PETALUMA   CA 94975

Pomegranate

EDWARD HOPPER (AMERICAN, 1882–1967)

Room in New York, 1932
Oil on canvas, 73.7 x 91.4 cm (29 x 36 in.)
Sheldon Memorial Art Gallery and Sculpture Garden,
University of Nebraska–Lincoln
UNL–F. M. Hall Collection

CA 94975   PETALUMA   BOX 808022

Pomegranate

EDWARD HOPPER (AMERICAN, 1882–1967)

East Wind over Weehawken, 1934
Oil on canvas, 86.4 x 127.6 cm (34 x 50¼ in.)
Courtesy of the Pennsylvania Academy of the Fine Arts,
Philadelphia
Collections Fund 1952.12

BOX 808022   PETALUMA   CA 94975

Pomegranate

EDWARD HOPPER (AMERICAN, 1882–1967)

Cape Cod Evening, 1939
Oil on canvas, 76.2 x 101.6 cm (30 x 40 in.)
John Hay Whitney Collection 1982.76.6

BOX 808022   PETALUMA   CA 94975

Pomegranate

EDWARD HOPPER (AMERICAN, 1882–1967)

Morning Sun, 1952
Oil on canvas, 71.4 x 101.9 cm (28⅛ x 40⅛ in.)
Columbus Museum of Art, Ohio
Museum Purchase, Howald Fund, 1954.031

BOX 808022   PETALUMA   CA 94975

Pomegranate

EDWARD HOPPER (AMERICAN, 1882–1967)

Drug Store, 1927
Oil on canvas, 73.7 x 101.9 cm (29 x 40⅛ in.)
Museum of Fine Arts, Boston
Bequest of John T. Spaulding 48.564

CA 94975

PETALUMA

BOX 808022

Pomegranate

EDWARD HOPPER (AMERICAN, 1882–1967)

Anderson's House, 1926
Watercolor over graphite pencil on paper,
35.4 x 50.7 cm (13¹⁵⁄₁₆ x 19¹⁵⁄₁₆ in.)
Museum of Fine Arts, Boston
Bequest of John T. Spaulding 48.720

BOX 808022   PETALUMA   CA 94975

Pomegranate

EDWARD HOPPER (AMERICAN, 1882–1967)

Apartment Houses, 1923
Oil on canvas, 61 x 73.5 cm (24 x 28¹⁵⁄₁₆ in.)
Courtesy of the Pennsylvania Academy of the Fine Arts,
Philadelphia
John Lambert Fund 1925.5

BOX 808022   PETALUMA   CA 94975

Pomegranate

EDWARD HOPPER (AMERICAN, 1882–1967)

Cottages at Wellfleet, 1933
Watercolor on paper, 50.8 x 71.1 cm (20 x 28 in.)
Private collection

BOX 808022   PETALUMA   CA 94975

Pomegranate

EDWARD HOPPER (AMERICAN, 1882–1967)

Two on the Aisle, 1927
Oil on canvas, 102.2 x 122.6 cm (40¼ x 48¼ in.)
Toledo Museum of Art 1935.49

CA 94975

PETALUMA

BOX 808022

Pomegranate

EDWARD HOPPER (AMERICAN, 1882–1967)

Captain Upton's House, 1927
Oil on canvas, 71.1 x 91.4 cm (28 x 36 in.)
Collection of Steve Martin

BOX 808022   PETALUMA   CA 94975

Pomegranate

EDWARD HOPPER (AMERICAN, 1882–1967)

Chop Suey, 1929
Oil on canvas, 81.3 x 96.5 cm (32 x 38 in.)
Collection of Barney A. Ebsworth

BOX 808022   PETALUMA   CA 94975

Pomegranate

EDWARD HOPPER (AMERICAN, 1882–1967)

Automat, 1927
Oil on canvas, 71.4 x 91.4 cm (28⅛ x 36 in.)
Des Moines Art Center Permanent Collections
Purchased with funds from the Edmundson Art
Foundation, Inc., 1958.2

BOX 808022   PETALUMA   CA 94975

Pomegranate

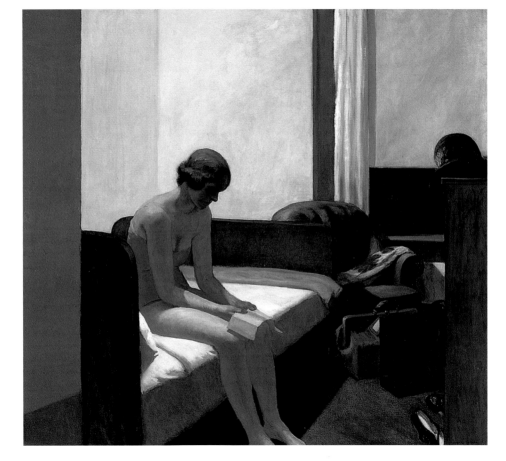

EDWARD HOPPER (AMERICAN, 1882–1967)

Hotel Room, 1931
Oil on canvas, 152.4 x 165.7 cm (60 x 65¼ in.)
Fondación Colección Thyssen-Bornemisza, Madrid

BOX 808022   PETALUMA   CA 94975

Pomegranate

EDWARD HOPPER (AMERICAN, 1882–1967)

Yawl Riding a Swell, 1935
Watercolor over graphite on paper, 51 x 71.8 cm (20⅟₁₆ x 28¼ in.)
Worcester Art Museum, Worcester, Massachusetts
Museum Purchase 1935.145

BOX 808022   PETALUMA   CA 94975

Pomegranate

EDWARD HOPPER (AMERICAN, 1882–1967)

Haskell's House, 1924
Watercolor over graphite on paperboard,
34.3 x 49.5 cm (13½ x 19½ in.)
Gift of Herbert A. Goldstone 1996.130.2

BOX 808022   PETALUMA   CA 94975

Pomegranate

EDWARD HOPPER (AMERICAN, 1882–1967)

Lighthouse Hill, 1927
Oil on canvas, 73.8 x 102.2 cm (29⅟₁₆ x 40¼ in.)
Dallas Museum of Art
Gift of Mr. and Mrs. Maurice Purnell

BOX 808022   PETALUMA   CA 94975

Pomegranate